ALL WOMEN ARE BITCHES

a handbook for men

by Will Hanson

SR
Stillwater
River

First Stillwater River Publications Edition

ISBN-10: 0-997-87780-4
ISBN-13: 978-0-997-87780-9

Library of Congress Control Number: 2016949432

2 3 4 5 6 7 8 9 10
Written by Will Hanson
Cover Design by Dawn M. Porter
Published by Stillwater River Publications, Glocester, RI, USA.

Publisher's Cataloging-In-Publication Data
(Prepared by The Donohue Group, Inc.)

Names: Hanson, Will, 1946-
Title: All women are bitches : a handbook for men / by Will Hanson.
Description: First Stillwater River Publications edition. | Glocester, RI, USA : Stillwater River Publications, [2016]
Identifiers: LCCN 2016949432 | ISBN 978-0-9978778-0-9 | ISBN 0-9978778-0-4
Subjects: LCSH: Sex differences (Psychology)--Humor. | Man-woman relationships--Humor. | Man-woman relationships--Religious aspects--Humor. | LCGFT: Humor.
Classification: LCC BF692.2 .H36 2016 | DDC 155.3/3--dc23

SPECIAL THANKS

Special thanks to the following people who provided valuable technical assistance and (or) positive feedback and encouragement during the writing of this book: Lindsay, Kali H., Matt, Jim, Cortney, Jason, Kali L., Melissa, Tom, Don, Mike, Linda, Lisa, Jon, Ron, Liz, Dawn and Steve.

It is greatly and sincerely appreciated.

INTRODUCTION

Years of dealing with women in various capacities has prompted me to try to understand and eventually analyze what the fuck is going on in their heads, and with their bodies. As crazy as this may sound to men, the actions of the more complex of the two genders can be relatively understood if viewed with a very open mind and from way outside the box. Guys, being inside the box distorts your ability to think clearly. If you haven't figured that out by now you should have. Ladies, if you do decide to read this, you will have to keep an open mind – way more open than it usually is.

I don't know why I waited so long but it wasn't until fairly recently that I decided to try to connect the dots and make some sense out of relationships and what is really going on between the sexes. And I don't mean in a superficial way either, I mean to dig deep and think hard. As it would appear that we were meant to have a partner, why is it so difficult to get along sometimes?

As the title states this is a book about "all women" but you will quickly realize that it's about all men, too. The focus however is clearly not on us; we're more like the victims. I didn't say that we were innocent victims, just victims.

As I plan to use some of my own life experiences, connections, and misconnections with women, I also plan to touch on a few historical events and delve much deeper than I should into the Bible and the Christian religion. It gets messy too but it's clearly relevant, so it's included.

The life experience chapters include factual events that happened throughout various stages of my life. Although officially considered to be fictional, much of the book is more like an autobiography. The religious and other chapters are obviously fictional and included for humor only.

I would hope that as you progress through these pages the contents will bring to mind examples of your own experiences. Whether female or male, you should have an abundance of them. If you don't, then you're either way too complacent, don't have a very good memory, or you just don't give a shit.

So like it or not, we're all in this together. I expect it will continue long after we're all gone, and new generations of women and men are born and try to figure out how to cohabitate and deal with each other through the trials and tribulations of life. So let's spend a little time to see if we can make it more tolerable. If that comment surprises you, then it's important that you're not mislead by the title of the book. Pay attention now because the whole point of this is to **try to bridge the gender gap,** gain a better understanding of each other, and bring us all closer together.

Yes, ladies, you read that correctly. I know it's not readily apparent in the title nor will it be in the first few chapters either. But bear with me and be patient. And if you haven't already figured it out from the title, what will become readily apparent is that I'm not into *polyticol corectnes*. I don't even know how to spell *polyticol corectnes* so don't look for it or expect to find it anywhere in the following pages or you will be greatly disappointed.

Chapter I

MOM BITCH

I'm sorry to say that I have to start with my mother. I know you're probably appalled but I got your attention, right? " All Women" obviously means mothers too, so it would be unfair of me not to include her. It would also totally contradict the purpose for which I chose to disclose the years of intentional and unintentional experiences and research that have led me to most of the conclusions in this book. I'll start with her because it was with her that I first started to notice that women had some stupid imbalances in their personalities. And one other reason – if she's not sacred, then as you will see, no one or no one's mother is sacred either, not even Jesus.

Granted no loving son should ever dare to call his mom a bitch, and I would have agreed a few years ago. I can assure you that I am a loving son and fully aware that this is a sensitive area but what the hell, let's get right to the point.

Please know up front that I have a very caring and loving mom and no one better mess with her son, no one but her. That's why this was so confusing to me at first. Let's start way back to when I was in the womb. I was really young then and don't remember much except that it was warm, dark, muggy, but overall a relatively good experience. The only problem I had was that there were about eight or nine periods of time before I popped out when I was very uncomfortable. It wasn't physical, but was more like an emotional discomfort. It would happen suddenly and with no warning. Very puzzling.

Now fast forward to when I was eleven- years-old and the first major incident that I can remember about my mom. It was an incident that has remained stuck in my craw and in my brain for all these years and one that I will never forget.

Like millions of boys before and after me, I lived and breathed for baseball. I'm not leaving out the girls but back then, as far as I knew, girls didn't play baseball. If they did, I didn't know any and there were no girls in

Little League. If that pisses you off, I'm sorry. Don't blame me, I didn't make the rules.

My dad was an avid baseball fan and student of the game. He was also a good teacher and began showing me the basics of the game when I was very young. At the age of nine I started playing in Little League and will never forget how excited I would get the days of the games and how I couldn't wait to get to the field. On this particular game day my mom, dad and I were having dinner and it appeared to be a normal, routine evening. It was a beautiful day, and it was a great night for a game. Like all good Italian families of the time (my mom is Italian), the main course was followed by the salad. I'm sure many of you reading this will remember that.

We had macaroni and meatballs that night which I loved. My mom made the best meatballs in the world. I know some of you think your mom makes or made the best meatballs but you're wrong. Your mom may be second best, though. Anyway, after finishing my macaroni and meatballs, I unknowingly made one of the biggest mistakes of my relatively young life. With my mind on the upcoming game, and in haste to finish my dinner, I politely asked for the salad and scooped

3

it into the empty spaghetti and meatball plate. That set off a chain of events I could never have predicted or understood at the time. My mom went fucking nuts on me and had this look on her face like she had just been bitten by a vampire. "What the hell is wrong with you and why didn't you wait for a clean dish? You should know better by now, you're not a damn baby! Who ever heard of putting the salad in a dirty dish?" And on and on and on.

OK, so I did do that but it was my dirty dish, my salad, and my decision. I didn't dare say that though out of respect and fear of having my fucking head knocked off. She was not going to let this go either. Something as horribly idiotic as this could not go unpunished so a majority of one, her, decided that I couldn't play in or go to the baseball game that night. I was in kid shock and my brain couldn't comprehend what had just happened. This was totally devastating to me not only because I would miss the game but because I had no idea what I did to warrant such a punishment or any punishment at all. I couldn't find any logic in her reaction or in her decision and I got that same uncomfortable feeling I used to get back in the womb.

There was another thing going on during this event that greatly troubled me, too. Like most children back then, I had two parents. One was obviously suffering from temporary insanity and the other was suddenly suffering from an inability to speak. My dad was sitting right there but he may as well have been in China. What was going through his mind and why didn't he say or do anything? A seemingly logical question at the time and one that took me quite a few years to answer.

So my dad went to the game without me (he was the manager). Instead of just letting me stay home, my mom took me to her girlfriend's house and made me hang with them all night. Could this get any worse? She was determined to pour salt in that wound for the entire night. *What a bitch!*

Chapter II

KEEPING IT
IN THE FAMILY

Although I will continue with another family example story, I would like you to understand that I really had a great childhood. I guess these just had more of a lasting impact on me because the people involved were very close to me.

My mom was one of seven children and had four brothers and two sisters. I loved them all and they were all very good to me as I was growing up and to my children as I continued to try to grow up. I have many years of very fond memories. All of her brothers were married and had children. Her two sisters were married but didn't have any children and I was an only child. It was like having three sets of parents. We were very close and did almost everything together – holidays, vacations, the beach, etc. They came to all my baseball games too when I was allowed to play. Was I spoiled? Yes. Was I a brat? I'll say no, I don't think so, well maybe, but I hope not. Because we were so close, I stayed many weekends and many summer days with my aunts and uncles and made some very good friends. Friends that I'm still very close to (seven friends, thirteen marriages).

So now I'm twelve-years-old and one day I'm staying with my aunt and uncle during the summer. It's a beautiful day, the sun is shining, the birds are chirping, and I was playing catch in the yard with my friend "Flip" (Phillip) the neighbor across the street. It was a great day to be a twelve-year-old, or so I thought. Boys or men should never get too comfortable though at any age. Like the Hurricane of '38, with no warning, my usually loving caring aunt opens the window and starts a rant that quickly cleared out all the chirping birds and hung a big dark cloud right over where I was standing. She had that same vampire face that my mom got sometimes and some pretty nasty shit came out of

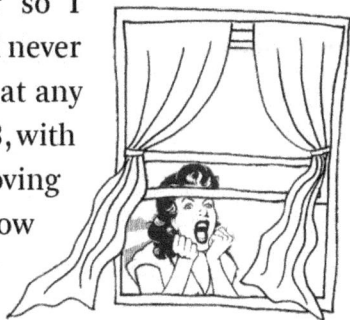

her mouth, too. "We never had any kids and I don't know why the hell we have to put up with you." Put up with me, but I was playing catch in the yard? "Your mother and father had the fun making you, they can have the fun taking care of you," and on and on and on. Remember, I was only 12 and I really didn't need to hear about the fun my parents had making me. It really made me uncomfortable. It still does.

I had no clue as to what to say or do so Flip and I just continued to play catch until she finally ran out of gas. I don't know if she got tired or embarrassed. By then all the neighbors seemed a lot more interested in what she was saying than I was, but I had that same womb feeling again.

What a bitch!

And once again I had no idea what I did to provoke such anger. I started to think there was something inherent in baseball that transforms women into raving lunatics. Obviously she was suffering from temporary insanity and my uncle was suddenly suffering from an inability to speak. He was there but he may as well have been in China. What was going through his mind and why didn't he say or do anything? Sound familiar?

Even though I was only twelve I began to see a very disturbing trend but still had no idea at the time what was really going on. I also started to question whether the male members of my family had testicles. I knew they did but where did they hide them during these troubled times and, most of all, why?

Chapter III

GENERAL STUFF

D on't think for a second as you read on that it's my intention to find a solution to this woman problem. There are no women or men alive, nor have there ever been, who could do that. I'm only planning to offer some insight and common ground to try to help us live through it and with it.

I have relayed two memorable experiences with loving relatives that occurred fairly early in my life and that started me thinking about all of this occasional turmoil. But there were many other female contacts, too – nuns, girlfriends, two wives, daughters, granddaughters, a great granddaughter, friends, and a female cat. Plenty more experiences, plenty more examples, but not yet.

All Women Are BITCHES

So as life and time went on, it became more apparent to me that the rib was truly the only thing that linked women to men. There wasn't much else that we shared either physically or emotionally. I also noticed that conflict usually originated with the females, and the males would generally just go along with it, or at least try to remain neutral. On those rare occasions when they didn't, the lady vampires would see to it that they would live to regret it. This is a very common practice among women and it made me realize that hiding ones' balls is really just a defense mechanism. It's not very masculine, but it's safer than daring to question or trying to interject any reasoning during these all too regular times of crisis.

OK, so the conflict origination comment probably pissed off most of you women, but I'm calling it the way I see it. Hang in there though, it will get more tolerable. And ladies, I know that at this point most of you know exactly where this is going. Gay men reading this do, too. They're more sensitive to stuff like this than non-gay men. And please don't go nuts thinking I have anything against gays. I am in total favor of that freedom of choice as long as they leave me alone and don't touch me. A hand shake or man hug is OK but that's it.

Most of the non-gay guys don't have a clue yet. They're just having fun reading this most likely during the commercials of a televised sporting event. They're probably drinking a beer and scratching their balls too if they don't have them hidden somewhere where they can't reach them.

Chapter IV

THE BITCH SCALE

Having established that all women are bitches, it's imperative that men understand the Bitch Scale. The Bitch Scale is similar to the Hot Scale with a couple of exceptions. As most of you know, the Hot Scale goes from 1 to 10. If a woman is super-hot, guys say she's a 10. The Bitch Scale is opposite of the Hot Scale and the lower the number, the better the score. The Bitch Scale goes from 1 to 11. One of the many duties of a parent is to educate. As a father, once I figured out the Bitch Scale, it was my duty to teach my two sons about it.

You're probably wondering why the Bitch Scale goes from 1 to 11 rather than from 1 to 10. It actually started out going from 1 to 10 until I was explaining it to my sons. They knew about the Hot Scale so I explained how the Bitch Scale works in reverse. "All women are bitches," I said. "The scale goes from 1 to 10. The trick is to try to find a woman who rates from 1 to 3. This is tolerable and will not leave you with any irreversible physical or psychological damage. If a woman is a 9 or 10 on the Hot Scale, you could consider going to a 4 on the Bitch Scale but at your own risk. Never, under any circumstances, should you go any higher than a 4."

My youngest son was paying very close attention and asked me where his mother was on the Bitch Scale. After careful consideration, the maximum Bitch Score changed from 10 to 11. She was there at the time, too. I'm ashamed to say that I used to hide my balls but not anymore, ever, or for any reason. We're not married any more. Just be aware that women expect you to hide your balls sometimes when it suits them and they're not horny. If you choose not to, like I did, there will most likely be consequences. Sometimes consequences are good!

Chapter V

BITCHES IN TRAINING

It's difficult to determine exactly when a female starts her bitch training, but it's at a very young age. I think it begins at age four. Prior to that they call it the terrible twos or terrible threes but they already have a name for it. There is actually a bitch gene which, like other genes, comes from the parents or in this case, the mothers. So right out of the womb women are born with a certain percentage of bitchiness. The rest comes from what they're taught by other women especially their mothers. If you're really serious about a woman get to know her mother, this might be a good indicator. I know you women hate that one too and you'll never admit it but it's true, deal with it.

The problem for men when trying to calculate where a woman is on the Bitch Scale is that we really can't pinpoint when she reaches her peak or highest score. It also varies in age and from woman to woman. The only advice I can give is to wait as long as possible because she will only go in one direction. It's like a good annuity, as the payments go up, they can stay where they are or go up more, but they will never go down. Guys, if you don't understand annuities, I'll simplify it for you. If a woman is a 3, she will never be a 1 or a 2, but there's no limit as to how high she can go. When you're evaluating her be sure to consider her age, how long you have known her, how much fluctuation you see in the upward direction, and how bitchy her mother is. If she's still moving up don't commit to anything. It's a judgment call that will affect your life forever.

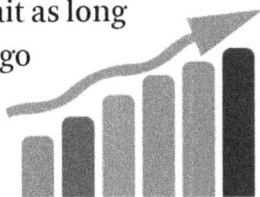

Chapter VI

THE ORIGINAL
BITCH

S o let's talk about Eve and the apple. All the pain, suffering, hate, anger, killing, famine, fires, floods and disease happened because EVE ATE THE FUCKING APPLE! That bitch had no self-control. Understandably a tough fact for all women to accept but an undisputed historical fact, no less.

I went through fourteen years of Catholic school and I'm fairly well versed in the Bible. There's a shit load of stuff in there that we're asked to believe solely on faith. It's stuff that really defies logic. Although I didn't dare question it at the time, I always wondered why God, with supposedly infinite wisdom, made a seemingly simple request of Eve, and why Eve couldn't stay away from the apple tree? God couldn't really tempt her with adultery because there were no other guys, Adam was the only guy around. But what was the big deal with the apple? Nothing, only that it was food. It could have been a peach, pear, or a fucking watermelon.

This is where we get into the real meat of the book and some eye opening facts. This is also where, with a heavy heart, I have officially broken away from church doctrine and have formulated a number of theories and assumptions that seem to make a lot more sense to me.

The Bible would have us believe that Eve was tempted by the devil in the form of a snake. A talking snake slithered up to her and told her that she would be like God if she ate the apple and she fell for it. Was Eve blonde? Is this bullshit or what? This had nothing to do with a devil or a fucking snake. God knew damn well (please pardon the pun) that Eve had PMS – the same PMS that has plagued women and men throughout the ages. The same PMS that causes women to have temporary insanity and look like vampires. The same PMS that takes all forms of logic out of any situation. The same

PMS that scares men into hiding their balls once a month when they know it's coming. God knew that no woman can pass up food or be told not to eat something when she has PMS. They will eat anything in site (well almost anything). I remember back to when my kids were babies, if my wife had PMS I was afraid to leave the house. I thought she would eat them and I would come home and find just bones.

So let's think about this original sin shit for a minute. A supposedly all loving God decided that all of mankind would be to blame and have to suffer and repent because a woman with PMS ate an apple. Are you fucking kidding me? God is supposed to be a fair, all just God too, so how does this make any sense? If the neighbor's wife kills her husband should your wife be arrested too? You might hope so but that's beside the point. It wouldn't be fair, right? So what's fair about original sin? God stacked the deck. This Paradise on earth thing was all a scam and was never meant to be. It was God's plan all along for us to go through this hell on earth. But why?

Chapter VII

GOD IS A WOMAN

Before we get into the details of this chapter, let me say that from this point forward I expect total understanding and respect from both genders toward the opposite gender. Now that we can discuss the details of what I think actually happened it will be clear that women are really not to blame for their bitchiness. That still doesn't make it any more tolerable for the men, but when women use that all too familiar phrase "**it's not my fault**," they're right. So guys, it's time for us to be more understanding and to give them a break. And ladies, it's time for you to do the same.

Your man, or men in general had nothing to do with inventing PMS so, in words I know you understand, **it's not our fault**, so you need to give us a break, too.

I know that some of you ladies have speculated for years that God was a woman and you were right. No man God would have been that vindictive or shot himself and all other men in the foot by giving women PMS. I hope you realize however that this really does nothing to get you more sympathy from the men. Sympathy no, understanding yes. And ladies please understand that most of what I'm referring to in the book is related to your monthly time of distress and not the rest of the month when you're "normal." You know what you're like and that's why some of you even let us know when you have it. It's short and not so sweet, "I'm PMSing" which when translated means "Whatever I do is not my fault, I'm giving you fair warning, and if you mess with me I'll fuck you up."

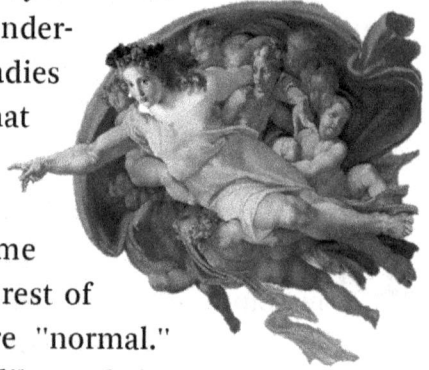

So I'm guessing that the week She spent creating all of this was the week before Her period.

God had PMS when She created us and that's why everything got so fucked up. Bad timing for mankind. So

She created Adam and looked at him and thought, "this guy looks too happy, let me pull out a rib." As there were no sedatives back then, that must have really hurt! Then she proceeded to create Eve. God with PMS was a hateful and vindictive God and had that malicious PMS venom flowing through Her veins. She really wanted to curse women and men forever. What better way than to create women in Her own image and likeness, PMS and all.

Women would suffer with it throughout the ages and torture men with it until the end of time.

Then a week later when Her PMS subsided, God decided to give us all a break and not let it last forever. She was more loving and compassionate and probably regretted making the PMS decision during Her time of discomfort (women always regret the shit they do when they have PMS but won't admit it). So She decided to end it when women got a little older and this would give both the women and the men a break and allow them to get along better in their later years.

That only lasted a few weeks until Her next cycle. Back came the PMS and She got bitchy again and decided to create menopause. Menopause is kind of like the frosting on the cake of PMS and would ensure some additional years of suffering for us all. This was also a total waste of God's time and energy. Once that womanly reproductive cycle begins, the PMS starts, and the approximate date of the month has been established, it's there forever. They're programmed. If you don't believe me, check it out. Pregnant women don't get periods so technically they shouldn't get PMS. Does the bitching go away for nine months? Hell no, sometimes they bitch more! Menopause or no menopause, it really doesn't matter. God help us!

Believe me when I tell you that a man God would have been more rational and thought this all through. Reproduction would have been much less complicated. She got the sex part right but why PMS and the bloody mess with periods and all the pain in giving birth? A man God would have made this all more of an easy going, less complicated, fun thing. He most likely would have created Adam, beer, and then a TV with a remote. Then He would have created Eve as an equal partner to get his beer and snacks for him. Man would reward her with sex which she would always want and never get enough of. There would be no such thing as a headache or a yeast infection and everyone would be happy. Oh, and do you really think a man God would have ever made sex a sin? No way, only for perverts and sex offenders (and why would anyone be stupid enough to offend sex?). All those guys would be immediately castrated and sent to the Paradise Jungle with plastic bags to pick up animal shit. Paradise on earth would also mean that we (adults) wouldn't have to work. Nature would supply almost every-thing we needed.

There would be no child labor laws and the children would make the beer, wine, and our favorite spirits. It would get them out of the house and out of our hair and teach them discipline. Anyway, that didn't happen and the rest is history, but it does leave a host of other serious unanswered questions that we will explore a little later in the book.

Chapter VIII

NUN BITCHES

I was taught by nuns for eight years. They could be a little bitchy too, sometimes. I had a nun in first grade that got really pissed at me for putting a tack on a girl's chair. The girl was cute and I wanted to get her attention. I was only six or seven at the time so how could the nun expect me to know the best way to get a girl's attention? Instead of just sitting me down and explaining it to me, she made me stand in the corner and called my mother and father, and they had to come to the school.

She also took my school tie away from me for one week because "I was unworthy of wearing it." Can you spell o-v-e-r-r-e-a-c-t-i-o-n? *What a bitch!*

I hated that tie anyway so that didn't bother me, but why does a nun have to fuck with a six-year-old? Apparently my mother understood why. Starting with that incident she told all my teachers during all my school years the same thing, "Don't be afraid to whack him if he doesn't behave and call me and I'll whack him when he gets home." And she meant it, and she did it. I got whacked a lot.

So the nuns would always tell us that they were married to God. If God is a woman, does that make nuns lesbians? I don't think the Supreme Court should go near that one, but more food for thought. And please don't go nuts thinking I have anything against lesbians. I am in total favor of that freedom of choice and they can touch me if they want to. OK, so I have a double standard regarding lesbians and gay guys. I think it has something to do with the software versus the hardware.

Chapter IX

HISTORICAL BITCHES

Although I think you're getting the point it would be unfair not to give dishonorable mention to some of history's most infamous bitches. The King (Elvis) even sang about a few who are in the Bible. Remember his song "*Hard Headed Woman*?" We already discussed Eve, but how about that Bitch Delilah? She nagged Sampson over and over to find the secret of his strength just so she could betray him to his enemies for money. The stupid bastard knew it too, and he still told her about his hair. She cut it off after he fell asleep in her lap (I'll bet face down), he lost all his strength, and the Philistines swooped in and captured him. How dumb was he? He could have used his strength to squash her like a fucking grape. Actually I think he did. She may have been in the temple when his hair grew back, his strength returned, and he destroyed it. Payback is a bitch!

Jezebel was one of the meanest, most miserable Bitches of all time and she wasn't even close to being hot. She was a ten on the Bitch Scale and only a one or two on the Hot Scale. So she marries King Ahab, screws up his head and has him worshiping pagan gods. As he was King of Israel, this didn't sit too well with the Jewish prophets. He had to be one of the biggest dickheads of all time too. How can a real guy let an *ugly* bitch ruin his life? And how did a stupid ass like that get to be a king? The Bible had a way of dealing with these bitches though. Jezebel was thrown from a tower and eaten by stray dogs. *Ouch!*

And then there was Cleopatra. She screwed up two guys lives that we know of (Julius Caesar and Mark Antony), but at least she was an eight on the Hot Scale. I can understand that a little more. And isn't it fitting that Liz Taylor got to play her in the movie. She was married eight times and Burton married her twice. Just getting married twice is dumb enough, but to the same woman? What the fuck was he thinking?

Chapter X

ANIMAL BITCHES

Bitches are not relegated only to humans. Animals share similar physiological and reproductive systems as humans, so the females have their own version of PMS and whatever else makes women occasionally nuts.

I have two male cats, Roo and Fang, who cohabitate very well. They are both indoor cats and one is actually a rescue cat that I took in about two years ago. He was wild and had no home so I would put food out for him and eventually adopted him and brought him into the house with the other male cat. In spite of having spent the first two years of his life outside on his own, he adapted quickly and, of course, the two males get along great. A lot like I do with my friends.

One of my granddaughters moved in about two years ago too and brought her female cat, Kit.

So I added two females to the household in one shot. Men should never do this regardless of the species. One female at a time is way more than enough and there should be a very long period of adjustment before considering adding another one (the only exception is if your girlfriend or wife has a twin).

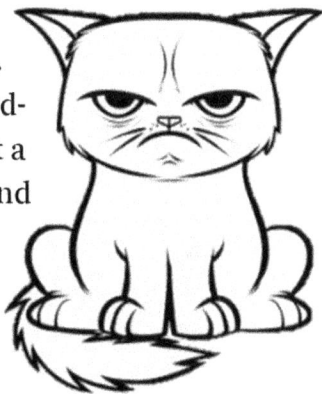

Needless to say, Kit gets bitchy and tries to terrorize my boys. She chases them, jumps on them and swats at them. She's breaking my house, too. She ruins the carpets, scratches the walls and rips the shower curtain liners. Fixing or replacing anything is useless because she'll only do it again. I don't have anyone over to my house anymore because I'm embarrassed. She sleeps under my bed at night and snores and I know she does it on purpose. She recently decided that she would chew through the cord of the ear buds I have for the radio in my bedroom (I need the radio to help me sleep because of all the stress in my life). She's like a fucking feline female terrorist but I put up with it because I love her, and I get more Heaven points.

Chapter XI

THE COVER GIRL

I will reluctantly conclude the examples with another very close relative. It's my beautiful seven-year-old great-granddaughter. She is adorable, smart, and an exception to the rules of bitch training. She actually started her training right after birth and right up to the age of two before she went through the terrible two's and three's. Then she picked up right where she left off on her fourth birthday. Look at the face, the picture tells it all.

It should go without saying that I truly love her but, as with my

mom, I have to tell it as I see it. Obviously she's way too young for this to be PMS related but there is a connection, hunger. When the urge to consume food kicks in, she transforms herself into an evil entity and the face automatically changes to the dreaded vampire face (I think all women have the same transforming face muscles). She loses complete control of anything that would resemble an adorable child, and when this happens she can out bitch some grown women that I know. The difference between her affliction and PMS is that five minutes after she eats, she's back to her adorable self. It doesn't last the mandatory five days like PMS but for that short period of time you can't tell the difference.

As a result of her premature training, I just hope I'm still alive when she gets older and gets her hooks into some poor un-expecting guy so I can at least warn him. I cringe at the thought of how high she can go on the bitch scale. I hope we don't have to create a new number just for her.

Chapter XII

THE HOLY TRINITY

So what about the Holy Trinity? When we thought God was a man, there were supposedly three persons in one God – the Father, the Son, and the Holy Ghost – and we're taught that they are equal. If they're equal, then how come the sign of the cross has one sign for The Father, one sign for the Son, and two signs for the Holy Ghost? What's equal about that and what the hell did he ever do anyway? His only claim to fame is the Immaculate Conception and knowing how to get a woman pregnant without sex. Am I missing something or did he leave out the best part?

So is there a Holy Trinity and, if so, what would they be called? How about the Mother, the Daughter, and the Holy Witch? I think they do exist but why haven't we heard anything from them and what about salvation? There are no accounts anywhere that I'm aware of about God sending Her only Daughter to save us from the fires of hell. They must have done something otherwise Limbo and Purgatory would be like overcrowded prisons. So what really happened? I know I'm treading on very sacred ground here, but please allow me to speculate on the possible events that may have led to an elaborate five female conspiracy, the most successful conspiracy in all of history.

The Mother went to the Daughter one day to explain Original Sin and how She needed someone to suffer and die for salvation. Expecting that the Daughter would feel some obligation to volunteer for this important assignment, She explained all the gory details of the Crucifixion but the Daughter was appalled and horrified. She was not really into pain and suffering, had nothing to wear to a Crucifixion, and knew that her hair and nails would get all messed up. So she started to cry and hyperventilate and proceeded to take the world's first hissy fit. After finally gaining her composure she looked at Her Mom and said "Mom, can't you get some guy to do it?" The Mother hesitated for a minute and said "Good idea, I'll send the Holy Witch down to earth to figure something out."

Chapter XIII

JESUS
AND THE APOSTLES

So if you believe in the possibilities raised in the last two chapters, then who was Jesus? Most likely he was a very good man but a pawn in the annals of creation who was manipulated into thinking he was the Son of God. My theory is that the Holy Witch conspired with Mary (his mom) to tell Jesus the Holy Ghost story about the Immaculate Conception and how she got pregnant by God without having sex (yeah right). When he was very young, he believed it. He probably started to have doubts as he got older and then puberty kicked in. Mary saw this as an opportunity, so now she conspired with Mary Magdalene and they came up with a plan. Mary M. would wash Jesus with her hair, tell him how wonderful it was that he had the Holy Ghost for a Father, and explain how special he was for being the Son of God. I have to admit that was a great plan. If a prostitute starts washing a man's body with her hair, he will believe anything she tells him. Men are weak that way, all of them. So now Jesus, thinking he was the Son of God, felt obligated to save us. He never really gave much thought to his hair and nails and he wore the same robe wherever he went.

I don't know about you, but I always had a problem with the theory of the Immaculate Conception. If your daughter, girlfriend or wife came home with that story would you believe it? I hope not, because you would be a dumb shit if you did. I think the apostles questioned whether or not Jesus was God, too, but they liked catching all those fish and getting the free bread and wine. Were these "miracles" though? Don't you think Houdini, Copperfield, or Franco could have done the same thing?

By the way, while we're on the subject, we all know the story about the Apostles falling asleep in the Garden of Gethsemane. If Jesus was really an all knowing God, and he wanted them to stay awake that night, why did he invite them for supper and give them copious amounts of wine?

I'm sure they were drinking it like it was water, too. Well it probably was water until just before they got there and Jesus changed it to wine. I wish I could do that. What, you really thought he did that only at one wedding? So anyway, they were probably drunk out of their minds when they left there. How did he expect them to stay awake?

The Apostles were like Jesus' crew. I have a crew but mine is smaller (there are only three of us) and I can understand how tight those guys were. A crew is like a band of brothers. If Jesus had Don and Mike in his crew, he would have had to learn how to change water into Grey Goose and Ketel One. Let me tell you something else about crew guys, they tend to get really into their crew chief and put him up on an imaginary pedestal, especially after they've had a few drinks. The stories they tell or gospels they write are greatly exaggerated and not very accurate. I don't know why they do that but they do.

If you're planning to have a crew, it helps to be sure that at least one of the crew members has a lot of money so you can vacation every year at South Beach. Jesus knew about this too, and that's why he had one or two tax collectors in his crew. I don't think they had any topless beaches back then though unless Sodom or Gomorrah was on the coast.

Chapter XIV

THE HOLIDAYS

The Holidays are always a special time for families, and for Christians, especially Christmas and Easter. I hope I didn't spoil that for you. I know it's difficult to absorb all of this as most of it goes against almost everything we were led to believe all of our lives. I had that same empty feeling when I first figured this all out but keep an open mind and don't get stressed. I'm not saying that we should totally disregard Jesus, I'm only saying that I don't think that he was God. He did suffer and die for us so we can still celebrate his birth. I'm still planning to attend Christmas Eve mass (if they let me) and get there early enough to listen to the choir. I really enjoy that and it's very inspirational. I wouldn't put too much faith in the Resurrection though, remember Houdini, Copperfield and Franco? We can keep Christ in Christmas but Santa and the Easter Bunny may now play an even more important role in these holidays than they did before. So remember all the gifts under the tree and the Easter egg hunt and get to the mall or on that computer and ring up those purchases. You'll be helping the economy too.

Speaking of Santa Claus and the mall, I should mention that I am a firm believer but I'm not too happy with him. He was at the mall about two weeks before Thanksgiving this past year and I'm at the mall almost every day walking to try to stay in shape. As I haven't been with a woman for a while, the mannequins were starting to look good to me, especially the ones at the Victoria's Secret store. I thought that was a little sick, so one morning I decided to talk to Santa and asked if he could bring me a woman for Christmas (and don't get any stupid ideas, I didn't sit on his lap). He said he would see what he could do but needed the necessary documentation. I went home and wrote him a detailed letter and gave it to him

the next day. We got pretty friendly over the next month and we would wave to each other when I walked by. I noticed his elves were very attractive so I stopped and told him that elves were acceptable because I hadn't specified that in my list. He said no that they were "private stock" but assured me that he was still working on my request. Christmas came and went and there were no women under my tree. I don't get mad. Sometime after the first of the year the following letter was sent to the North Pole:

Dear Mrs. Santa Claus,

Santa is screwing around with the elves at the Mall. Just thought you should know.

Your friend,

Will

Chapter XV

RELIGION

Although many of the thoughts, comments, and conclusions in this book are based on my own Christian religious background, it is not my intention to neglect, ignore, or disregard any of the other religions. There are many, and I'm not going to try to name them for fear of forgetting a couple and pissing some people off. I wouldn't want that to happen! The true one, I guess, is the one you really believe in.

Some people don't believe in any religion, and although I'm keeping an open mind, I'm not ready to go to a place where there is no life after death. If everyone believed that then the world would be more fucked up than it is already. The fear of some sort of hell at least keeps most of us in line. And I do believe in Hell (but not in the Devil) because there has to be a place for murderers, rapists, and people who hurt kids, women, and animals. For the rest of us I think our hell is here on Earth. I choose to believe in Heaven because I think we all want to see the relatives, friends and pets again that we loved during our lifetime. If some of the assholes we really didn't like too much make it there, then I guess we can just ignore them or at least hope they live in a different neighborhood.

So is Heaven really Heaven when God has PMS? Yes, and I have a theory about that too. I already told you that I don't believe in the Devil. To truly reward those of us who make it to heaven and to not have to deal with Her wrath, I think God leaves Heaven and goes to Hell when She has PMS to deal with the inmates there. It's a good plan and let's face it, no Devil could raise Hell with the sinners any better than a God with PMS. I'll bet She really fucks with them, too. When She returns to Heaven She makes them watch a DVD of Herself bitching at them and puts the volume up full blast until She goes back the next month. Trust me sinners, you don't want to go there, so turn your life around before it's too late.

Church could be a problem for me now. Although I go every week, I'm not sure if they will let me into a church after they find out I wrote this book. If not, I may have to do TV mass like I do when I'm sick or hungover from another great Saturday night on Federal Hill. That means no communion either but I guess I can do my own bread and wine. I won't pretend to be changing it into anything though. Be honest, if you really thought it was flesh and blood would you be eating and drinking it? The lady vampires might, but I wouldn't. We'll see if the priest has a sense of humor or if they'll make me register as a church offender and stay 500 feet away from all the churches. That would suck be- cause one of my favorite restaurants is only about 300 feet from a church.

By the way, not that it's relevant, but there are still some parts of the Bible that I agree with like, "an eye for an eye." If I wrote the Bible I would have made it "two eyes for an eye." We wouldn't be wasting all the time and money with trials either. If you kill somebody, we kill you, revive you, and kill you again. Oh, I'm sorry, do you think I lack compassion? Let me guess, it's not your fault it's your mother's fault. When you were a kid, she traumatized you by making you miss a few baseball games for no good reason so you became an axe murderer. That's bullshit, suck it up. If you're really that angry, try writing a book, it's good therapy.

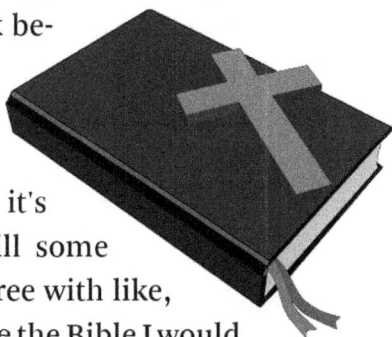

While we're on the subject of murderers, and to prove I have compassion, I'm inclined to give Cain a pass for killing Abel. Another God thing that I'm questioning but at the time there were no Commandments. Siblings fight all the time and maybe this got out of hand but I blame God for that. She waited thousands of years before giving the Commandments to Moses. The poor guy was about 80 and had to fast 40 days and 40 nights in the desert before She would give them up too. That's fucked up. The commandments should have been nailed to a palm tree before she created Adam. She should have known that!

Chapter XVI

YOU CAN'T LIVE WITH THEM

You know the saying about women, "You can't live with them and you can't live without them." I can tell you from experience that you can easily do either one. Men, it's your choice to make but whatever the choice, make the most of it. Being married or living with a woman is great if you have the right woman and if your relationship is open, honest, and you share a mutual respect for each other. The golden rule works well and should always be the benchmark. If not, get the fuck out.

Keep the Bitch Scale in mind and don't get sucked in or you will have a living hell. The only upside to this is that while you're living this hell you accumulate Heaven points. Some guys get more Heaven points than they need and can share the surplus with their friends. I'm sharing mine with my crew (they need them). Be ever mindful of your situation and what it can do to you if you choose to settle. Things can change quickly on you too, so always expect the unexpected. Let's take a hypothetical situation where you have a woman high on the Bitch Scale at home but think you can deal with it. What about work? Suppose some day you find yourself with a woman boss who is also high on the Bitch Scale? One at home and one at work. You're screwed and will throw up a lot. As I said, this is hypothetical.

Watch out for those women who try to steal your brain too. They might all do it but I'm not sure.

You may not have thought of it in those terms but at least some women will attempt to make you void of any thoughts, ideas or opinions unless they're exactly like their own. Because women know that they're always right they can't comprehend how anyone can be stupid enough to disagree with them. A few examples might be helpful.

Example 1:

If she dislikes someone, then you have to dislike them too. Staying neutral is totally unacceptable and you have to dislike that person at least as much or more than she does. Hating them will keep you out of trouble and may even get you some well needed points with her. If you can't bring yourself to do that please, whatever you do, don't ever go as far as to say "I think you may be over-reacting." This will put you in very deep shit, deeper than you can ever climb out of. You may even wish you suffocated in the shit rather than deal with what she'll put you through for saying that.

Example 2:

You wake up on a Saturday or Sunday during the summer and it's a beautiful day. You work during the week so you're thinking about all you can accomplish in your yard. Your woman wakes up and says "Beautiful day to go to the beach." You are now totally fucked and in a lose/lose situation. You're not only thinking about all the work you have to do but you're really not in the mood to sit in all that traffic or drive your clean car through the dusty parking lot at the beach. She already knows that and that's why she set you up. She has you right by the balls, too. Are you going to say "No, I have work to do?" Good luck with that because that's not an option if you know what's good for you. So you decide to be a loving partner and go to the beach but make the mistake of telling her that you had planned to get some things done around the house but will go to the beach instead. Not good enough. She has determined that it's a perfect beach day. The house and yard work can wait and she doesn't understand why you can't see that. "Don't do me any favors," she says and now you pissed her off. As I said, you're totally fucked. She wants your brain to think like her brain and nothing short of that will satisfy her.

Example 3:

Now let's take that same day, same conditions. You wake up and say to her "Beautiful day to go to the beach." She looks at you with that face and says "Are you nuts? We work all week and there's a ton of work that needs to be done around here. Do you think the grass is going to cut itself? There's no way I'm going to the fucking beach today." So what just happened? Simple, going to the beach was your idea that came from your brain not her brain. Her brain just woke up and didn't have a chance to decide what it wanted to do but was smart enough to know that any idea that came from your brain sucked.

The point is that you may be faced with a situation. Do you want a woman, or do you want your own brain? The problem is that men have the "vagina syndrome" and like having one close by even if they rarely see it. Not all guys realize it but all the women do. They know that it's the strongest hole in the universe because it carries more weight with men than the slaves who built the pyramids.

You know that Eve ate the apple but at that point only the women were on God's shit list. Adam still hadn't done anything to piss God off which really bothered Eve. She had to figure out a way to get Adam to eat an apple too. She knew that Adam had the vagina syndrome so it wasn't rocket science. She never said a word to him either, she just put the apple between her legs and he was on it before she could blink. Guys, we need to be smarter. How much shit you want to endure is up to you, but just remember, there are options. If you really need something, you can always get a blow up doll.

Chapter XVII

COMPARING WOMEN TO BLOW UP DOLLS

N ever mind, this might be too offensive. Use your imagination.

Chapter XVIII

THANK YOU, ALBERT EINSTEIN

O ne of the primary causes of guys getting bitched at over the years has been our refusal to stop and ask for directions when we're driving. Women have depended on it for decades as a way to release PMS venom. Why do you think they ask us if we just want to go for a ride sometimes? Now you know.

Developments in technology have made this all but extinct except for guys who can't afford GPS and are still too stupid to realize that the five minutes it takes to stop and ask for directions is much better than the alternative hours of shit they have to deal with. Now Einstein didn't actually invent the GPS so why is there a chapter of the book dedicated to him?

Roger Easton, Ivan Betting, and Bradford Parkinson seem to be getting the credit for inventing the GPS, but when I researched it and dug a little deeper, it took me in a totally different direction.

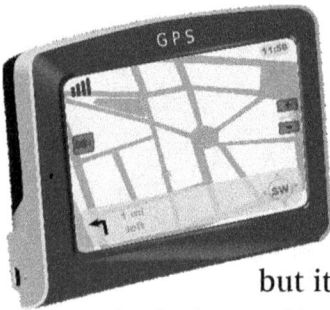

GPS operates with a number of signals bouncing off multiple satellites and a series of complicated equations. I'm not trying to explain or pretend that I understand it, but it also relies on time and gravity calculations. If it wasn't for Einstein's "Theory of Relativity," GPS would not have been possible. I had a feeling there was more to this than met the untrained eye and it was probably worth the time to dig a little deeper. What I wanted to know is why Einstein developed the Theory of Relativity and what was his motivation?

Einstein was born in Germany in 1879 and was obviously a very intelligent and curious child. In 1886, German inventor Karl Benz built the first gas powered automobile. This was a major technological break-through and one that would have made international headlines. It also would have captured the imagination of a very bright, scientifically gifted seven-year-old. I think that it was this invention that lead to Einstein's "Theory of Relativity."

As Albert got older, so did the advancement of automobiles and his interest and fascination with them grew, too. Albert knew how to think way outside the box which was amazing because thinking outside the box wasn't even invented until the 1980's. Einstein had other Theories and had written papers on light, atoms, and energy but with his fascination of automobiles came some concerns. Albert could look well into the future and could see a recipe for disaster. Here was a machine that could transport a small number of people for unknown distances. It was much smaller than a jail cell and some-what confining. He knew it would be used primarily to transport the owner but also the owner's wife or girl-friend, or both (but not at the same time). Now Albert never got lost going anywhere, he was too smart. But his friends would tell him horror stories about getting lost with the horse and buggy and getting bitched at by their girlfriends or wives for not stopping for directions. It was said that for his theory on light, he would actually imagine himself riding on a beam of light. If he could do that

I guess it was easy for him to imagine himself riding in a car with a woman bitching at him. He knew a GPS would solve the problem but could only be invented if someone discovered "Relativity" first. As a result, he dedicated most of his future efforts to this discovery. I call this "Will's Theory of Einstein's Theory of Relativity." So from guys everywhere, thank you Albert and also Roger, Ivan and Brad!

Please note that as was the case with Einstein, many of the chapters in this book are also based on theories, my theories. His theories were rebuked and discounted for years until proven to be true and then he was regarded as a genius. I will tell you that I am no genius but that doesn't mean that my theories are wrong. I guess we'll see if they stand the test of time.

And just for the record I happen to think guys get a bad rap for doing this because women do it too. Don't you think Amelia Earhart wishes she had stopped for directions?

CHAPTER XIX

THE REVELATION

So let me now tell you about my "greatest" single life experience. The one that forced me to deal with the PMS plague like no man should ever have to. The one that really prompted me to draw conclusions like the ones I have shared with you in this book. The one that, along with my second wife, got me so many extra Heaven points.

I had a job as a facility manager for a local manufacturing company. Although like many other companies they had downsized quite a bit, there were still about 150 employees who remained. Conservatively, about 80 of them were women. So do the math. On average, about 20 women in that facility had PMS every day.

If they averaged an 8-hour day, that's 160 woman hours of PMS daily that was spread out all over that facility. That's 160 hours they so generously shared with me. Guys, think about it, you know the hell you go through for that week. But think about 160 hours of it every day with relief only on weekends. And I still had to deal with the usual shit at home. You know the first thing on a woman's mind when she has PMS is busting some guy's balls. When she's home, that's you. When she was working, it was me.

As I was responsible for heat, air conditioning, security, meeting room set-ups, moves, maintenance, janitorial services, and the parking lot, I had the privilege of hearing from many of them on a daily basis. I got really good at identifying whether they had PMS or not, too. If it was a personal visit, I would always look for that face that my mom and aunt had back when I was very young. We're in a new millennium now, but the look is still the same. If it was a phone call, I could tell within the first two or three words just by the attitude and the tone. I couldn't see the face but I knew the look was there, too. I preferred the phone because as difficult as it was sometimes, I tried to be cordial. On the phone

though I could make my own faces and they couldn't see me. The truth is, I really didn't give a shit about their problem whether they had PMS or not. Honestly, what am I supposed to do when one calls and says she's too hot, and another one calls and says she's too cold, and they sit next to each other? The only solution is for one to take off all her clothes, or the other one to put on a fucking sweater, or both. Obviously I couldn't say that but it did teach me discipline and tact and a fair amount of bullshit. We're never too old to learn!

There was one lady who is a really good person but that didn't stop her from being a woman. She also had the most acute sense of smell of any human being, ever. When I saw her name on my caller ID I would cringe. "Will, I smell gas." If the wind was blowing in the right direction, and a mosquito farted in the next town over, she could smell it. I knew what it was but I couldn't tell her that so I would thank her for bringing it to my attention. Then I would walk around the facility especially in her area so she could see me and think I was trying to solve her problem. I was really just praying for the wind to shift and for my 160-hour day to end.

And then there was this one. I got a call that one of the toilets in the ladies' room was clogged so I went to check it out and asked one of our maintenance employees to try to unclog it. Generally, this is something they can do fairly easily but this one was too severe so we had to pay to get an outside plumber.

After he was in there for about an hour and tore all the pipes apart, I got a call saying that he found the problem. I went to the ladies' room and he was standing there with a pair of women's panties that he pulled from deep into the piping. Being analytical, I tried to find a rational reason for this and not jump to the conclusion that some bitch did this on purpose. My thought process was as follows: so unlike men, when women go they have to sit down regardless of the reason. The panties have to be pulled down I would think to a location somewhere around the ankles. Normally they would stay in place or possibly drop down a little and, giving the benefit of the doubt, maybe even somehow get past the shoes and onto the floor. I couldn't find any scenario where they could actually do all that and then accidently jump from the floor into the toilet, especially without the person noticing. So I concluded that the bitch did it on purpose because she was most likely PMSing. Her motive was to drive me nuts by having to shut down the ladies' room, which would piss off more women, and screw up my budget by having to spend money to get it fixed. The only thing I didn't know was if she had PMS before she went to the ladies' room, which would have made it premeditated, or if it came on all of a sudden while the princess was on her throne. Can you believe this shit?

Because I was also responsible for security, I was determined to find out who did this and I had a foolproof plan. Remember Cinderella and the slipper? I wanted to get all the women together to try on those panties until I found the ass that fit them. But when I asked my boss, he wouldn't let me do it. I still regret not being able to do that. Instead the bitch got away with the perfect panty crime. Five years later she's probably still gloating over it and it still burns my ass that she got away with it.

Chapter XX

THE OTHER PMS

There is another little known, never talked about variety of PMS. I don't like to keep picking on my second wife, but I only discovered it after I met her. There is the PMS everyone knows about (pre-menstrual syndrome) and then MS (menstrual syndrome) and that's where it ends for the month for most women. A small percentage of the female population gets the other PMS (post-menstrual syndrome) after the MS. The side effects are exactly like the first PMS and it lasts the same amount of time. If you figure it out, PMS lasts about five days, MS about five days, and another 5 days for those who get the second PMS. So now you killed half the month. And that's assuming that nothing else will happen to screw up the other half. I don't care how hot she is, it's not worth spending half of your life getting bitched at. I wonder if God gets the other PMS?

Chapter XXI

BEING PRO-ACTIVE

So guys, you might want to consider being pro-active as a way to combat the monthly aggravation.

Fortunately, PMS is on a fairly regular schedule. She knows when it's coming and if you're anything like I was you have the date etched in your brain like your birthday. Women have it all planned out and know from years of experience that they can aggravate the shit out of us and we will most likely back

down or they'll just make it worse. Try a different approach. Next month when you know it's getting close, hang your balls right out of your pants so she can see them. Stand right up to her and I guarantee this will take her totally by surprise. Then one of two things will happen:

1. She will stop bitching at you because she will gain a new respect and admiration for you and realize the days of you hiding your balls are over.

2. She'll head for the nearest kitchen knife.

If she heads for the knife tuck your balls back into your pants and run and don't ever come back.

Even if she tries to contact you and tell you everything is OK, don't believe it, she will mess you up. She'll wait for you to fall asleep and cut your balls right off. Some women actually fantasize about doing that.

Guys who don't have one woman in their life, like me, have to use a different approach. You never know who you might meet or when, or where they are in their cycle. I hang my balls out 24/7 (figuratively of course) so right from the beginning there are no misunderstandings. You should be aware, however, that if you do this, you could be alone forever.

Chapter XXII

Paying for Sex

O K, Don Juan, this chapter is for you and all the macho, naive idiots who brag about never paying for sex. The rest of you can skip it and go right to the next chapter.

Listen carefully you dope: if you ever had it, you paid for it. Paying for it doesn't just mean handing over money to a prostitute. There are hundreds and maybe thousands of ways you're paying and you don't even know it. Women have their own handbook for this and no man has ever seen it. It was written by women, for women, and as soon as a woman reaches the age of eighteen there is a ceremony much like a Mafia induction. And please don't go nuts thinking I have anything against Mafia guys. I told you my

mom is Italian and for the sake of my overall well-being I will tell you that I love all my *Paisans* and they're actually helping the economy, too. Think about all the law enforcement people who would be on the unemployment list if it wasn't for them. So it's at this induction where the bitch in training is given the handbook and sworn to secrecy. They can never mention it to a man or they will both disappear and never be seen again. That's why there are so many unsolved missing persons' cases. They have a hit squad for this which is the female version of Murder Incorporated.

Anyway, the BIT is given a certain amount of time to memorize the list and after they do, there is another ceremony where they're tested. If they pass, the book is destroyed (I think they burn it). That's why you have never seen it and probably didn't even know about it until now. Then they go through their whole lives and never forget a single thing on that list. Even when they get older and the memory starts to go, Alzheimer's sets in and they can't even remember their own name, they still never forget that fucking list.

So from now on, keep your mouth shut about not paying for sex. It makes you look stupid and women think that all men are stupid so you're just fueling their fire.

Chapter XXIII

ALL MEN ARE BASTARDS

I won't bother to elaborate on this, but in addition to being sons of bitches, all men are bastards. We know it, and we don't care. It's the only defense mechanism we have and, admittedly, it's not a very good one. We can't even come close to competing but I guess it's better than nothing.

I'm sure one of you women would love to write your own book about this, so be my guest. I'll read it but keep in mind that you won't be telling us anything we don't already know (I don't think I told you anything you didn't already know either). If you do decide to write about us though, please don't say anything that may drive a wedge between the two genders. After all the work I did trying to bridge the gap and heal the wounds I would hate to see anything come between us now.

And ladies, if we're really that bad, why do you outlive us? My very good friend John always tells me that men die first because they want to. I thought that was funny until I started to think about it. He may be right about that!

Chapter XXIV

THE CONFESSION

So what's really behind all of this? What prompted me at this stage of my life to sit down and write a book? Do you think it was my desire to help mankind? That I felt some philanthropic need to bring women and men closer together? If you do, then you probably believe the Immaculate Conception story and you're a dumb shit.

Have you ever watched the TV show *Californication*? About eighteen months ago, I started

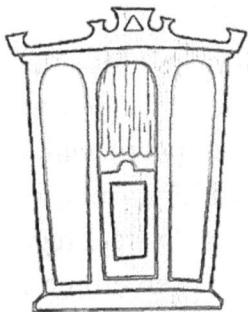

watching it on Netflix. The character Hank Moody was my inspiration to sit down and start writing. I'm amazed at his ability to attract women. He gets more women than the Rat Pack and spends a lot more time in bed with them than he does writing. There is apparently something about writers that drives women absolutely crazy so I decided to become a writer.

So ladies, if you think you might be interested, please let me know. I don't want to discriminate but please be very low on the Bitch Scale (see Chapter IV). Not that I put much faith in your self-assessment, but it's a place to start. And to make it easier for you, allow me to mention a few other preferences.

You and I know that there are guys whose only requirement in a woman is a functional vagina. Beyond that, they really don't care. That's on my list too but it's not the only thing I care about. I'm slightly more complex than that. Although I'm open to women of all races, I am partial to non-white women, especially Latin women with the Jennifer Lopez asses. They're so hot!

I'm looking for someone to love and for sex and don't mind if it's the same person. And I have just two other simple requests: 1) I don't want anyone who can beat me up so please, no lady boxers, kick boxers, wrestlers, biker women or women who know karate regardless of the belt color. 2) No "heavy" women either. Not that I don't think heavy women are attractive or hot, but I like to get on the bottom sometimes and they might hurt me.

And I shouldn't have to say this but if you're married or have a friend, forget it, I don't go there. No cheating! And don't try to justify it because you can't. And that goes for the guys too. If you have something good do everything you can to hold on to it. If not, go out and find it, you owe it to yourself.

Chapter XXV

THE FUTURE?

I'm still trying to figure out what to do when I grow up, but for now, maybe this book will make me famous and the *Today Show* or *CBS This Morning* will call me. I would love to get a chance to meet Norah O'Donnell. She's a definite 10 and the hottest chick on the planet except for Amanda, Yinny, Sabrina, Liz, Lea, Tori, Bianca, Jess, Molly, and Brianna. I'm trying to convince myself that she's only a 1 on the bitch scale, too. That combination is very rare among women. And yes, I know she's happily married but I can look and not touch. I look all the time (about fifty to a hundred times a day) but I'm out of touch with touching. Just looking can be a problem too, though, if you're not good at identifying the body language when they look back. I was checking one out at the mall the other day (a live one, not a manne-quin) and she gave me a look back. I couldn't tell if it was "come and get it, it's all yours" or "what the fuck are you looking at?" Being somewhat conservative, I figured it was safer to just walk away. If you're more daring there is something else you could consider. My good friend and crew member Mike tells me all the time to, "throw it out there." He says, "go for it because what's the worst that can happen? They say no and think you're an asshole. They probably thought you were an asshole anyway before you even opened your mouth." Words of wisdom.

Mike shares many words of wisdom about women with me but his most recent is my favorite. "Will" he said, "stop looking for Cadillacs and settle for a few Volkswagens. The ride might be a little bumpier but they will still get you where you want to go." Wow, who thinks like that? I guess he spends a lot of time thinking about women.

I wonder if *Saturday Night Live* might call me to host a show? They love having crazy people on that show but I don't think they pay too well. I might make an exception for them though.

OK, so neither of those things will happen, but I didn't write this for fame, I wrote it for the money. Young women are fun but they're expensive and I need to supplement my fixed income. Please tell your friends about the book but **don't share your copy with them**, make them buy their own. Thanks!

By the way, speaking of SNL, I used to always watch it in my younger years but I never stay up that late any more unless I'm at the bar with The Angels. Steve Martin is one of my all-time favorite comedians. Steve said that to be funny you have to feel funny. I thought I would try to feel funny when I started writing this book but the feeling quickly escalated to fucking insanity! Sometimes it felt like an out of body experience where my Royal typewriter was typing on its own and I had no control. That may be normal for writers, but how would I know? I don't know if there's a market for insanity but I guess we'll find out.

Rowling, Shakespeare, Poe, Paterson and the rest of you need not worry about the competition though. Writing more books is not on my bucket list and this one wore me down and fried my brain so I need to rest.

So what's really next for me? I was considering detective work so that I could help solve some of the missing persons cases. Now that we have a motive and a new line of evidence to follow, it shouldn't be too difficult. I'm afraid, however, that the same hit squad that made

all those people disappear will make me disappear too,
so I reconsidered.

Chapter XXVI

THE PMS DEFENSE

I f you're a woman and actually took the time to read this book I feel like I owe you something. I'm sure there are many women who saw the title and said "Fuck this asshole, I'm not reading this shit." Too bad because they will never get to appreciate the literary value. They won't get the benefit of this helpful advice either.

In criminal cases we have all heard about the temporary insanity plea, which is seldom used because it doesn't get very positive results. With all the high IQ lawyers who have been around forever, I really don't understand why no one has thought of this sooner, but how about the PMS plea? Prosecutors, judges, defense attorneys, and especially juries are obviously made up of women and (or) men. All women know they're insane when they have PMS and all men know they're fucking nuts too. So, if you commit a crime, no jury in the world is going to convict you as long as you can prove you were pre-menstrual. And I shouldn't tell you this, but if you're planning to commit a crime, just wait for the PMS.

Hey, maybe I could start practicing law as a defense attorney and you could hire me if you need one. It would only be fair as this was my idea, right? And I can be very flexible so if you don't have any money, I'm sure we can work something out.

I might be busy though as I'm seriously considering acting next. A movie with De Niro, Pacino, and Pesci would be fun. I would like to get the lead role though and Jennifer Lopez as my hot Latin lover. If she's not available then maybe Cameron Diaz. She looks white to me but she has a Latin name. Does anyone know how I can contact any of these people? I don't have an agent.

I'm sorry to say I may have to put this on hold for a while. Football season is approaching and I can feel an itch coming on and I have to get to the liquor store.

In closing, my sincere thanks to everyone who took the time to read this. Be good to yourselves and to your family, friends, lovers and pets.

EPILOGUE

THE CREW

You're probably asking yourself why is there an Epilogue written about the crew? I asked the same question so let me try to explain.

When you write a book it is recommended that you have as many people read it as possible to get constructive feedback before trying to get it published. That was especially important to me as this was my first book and I was very open to any suggestion. The manuscript went to friends, relatives, males and females, and people who didn't know me. I probably should have been a little more selective as to who I sent it to though, and asked my crew, Don and Mike, to read it.

In spite of his busy schedule, Mike got on it right away and got back to me within a few days. He told me that it was the best book he had ever read. That would normally be a great compliment except that it may well be the only book he ever read. The only thing I ever saw him reading was a menu. Don didn't get back to me for weeks because he couldn't open the file. He's technically challenged but won't admit it. Judge for yourself, he forgot his password. He has a master's degree, too, but obviously not in computer science.

So why am I telling you this? Instead of commenting on the contents of the book, the best they could come up with was that their feelings were hurt because they weren't mentioned more in it. I would have thought that the title, "All Women Are Bitches," would have been somewhat of an indication that the book really wasn't about them. As a result of their feedback however I decided to devote a section of the book to them. A good crew chief should let his crew think they're important whether he thinks they are or not.

I also decided to seize the opportunity to tell them publically that they need to show a little more respect for their chief. As an example, some time ago, Don told us that he got engaged. So now Mike starts sucking up to him and Don absorbs it like a sponge. Mike knows that he's vulnerable because he really doesn't have many friends. So then Don asks Mike to be the best man at his wedding and asks the chief if he wants to be the ring bearer. Very fucking funny! That probably would have bothered me more but Don's engagements last longer than the life expectancy of most animals. Given Mike's life style, who knows if he will even be around by the time there's a wedding? Don't get me wrong, I hope he is, but I may be the best man and the ring bearer.

OK, I feel better now.

Don and Mike, I hope you feel better too now that you have a section of the book devoted just to you. And thanks for the feedback.

EPILOGUE to the EPILOGUE

On May 17, 2017 our great friend Don suffered an aortic dissection, the separation of the outer layers of the artery carrying blood from the heart. He was rushed to the hospital and went through a seven hour surgery. Needless to say this was very serious and he was close to death. Two and a half weeks of his life went by before he regained consciousness but he fought hard and continued to improve (I think mainly because he wanted to see me again). Finally after three and a half weeks in the Critical Care Unit, and two and a half weeks at rehab, he was released and sent home. A real tribute to his stamina, strength, and will to live.

Physically, they expect a full recovery. Mentally he's good but the doctor thinks he has some issues as a result of minor strokes he suffered during his ordeal.

The doctor says he's at about 85% mentally but will eventually get back to normal. Mike and I hope he stays at 85%. The doctor probably doesn't realize that he was only at 75% before he got sick.

Welcome back Don, it's great to have the full crew back together again.

ACKNOWLEDGEMENTS

Thanks to my family and friends and cats who help keep me going. I love you guys!

Roo and Fang, this isn't going to sit well with some of the guys, but you're my two best friends.

First wife, from what I can remember, I don't think you were very high on the Bitch Scale. I guess I was high on the Bastard Scale back then though. Sorry!

Second wife, thanks for being a "good sport" about this book.

Jim, you always said I do a good job of walking the fence without falling off. How about now?

Poochy, Anthony, John, Ron, and Ray, it's been great for many years. I hope we get many more and I miss Ernie too.

All Women Are BITCHES

Melissa, Lindsay, Cortney, Kali, Courtney, Taylor, Tori, Gabrielle, Angelina, Avery, and Bailey, please don't be offended.

Matt, you probably won't endorse this book but don't be mad at me for writing it.

Jason, I know you love it.

Amanda, Yinni and Sabrina, love you, thanks for hanging out.

Lea, Tori, Bianca, Jess, Molly and Brianna, there are only three guys I know who were fortunate enough to have Angels while they were still alive, George Bailey, Charlie, and Will. George's angel was a guy and Charlie only had three. Thanks, love you!

Liz, please put the heart back on my beer foam, LY.

Pete, you were dealt a bad hand but have impressed a lot of people with your continuous hard work and great attitude. We're proud to have you as a friend.

Don and Mike: what happens in the fucking crew, stays in the fucking crew. You should try getting your own

Heaven points and don't just rely on the extra ones I gave to you. Please don't write any gospels about me when I'm gone either or I might resurrect just to haunt you. And always remember, our lips are sealed.

Will

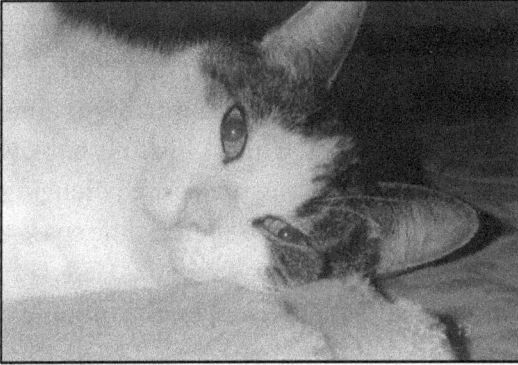

Roo died on July 22nd, 2016 and was a beloved member of our family for over twelve years.

He gave us much love and happiness in return and will remain in our hearts and minds forever.

ABOUT THE AUTHOR

Will Hanson is a Rhode Island native retired from manufacturing management where he worked for one company for almost forty-six years. This is his first book which he decided to write as a challenging but enjoyable way to spend some spare time and for other reasons mentioned in the book. He loves golf but hates his handicap and spends most of his time with family and great friends including his two cats.

Will is a member of The Association of Rhode Island Authors and lives with his daughter and granddaughter in Rhode Island.